# 200[

# PRESIDENTIAL

# ELECTION

## RICHARD J. SEMIATIN
*American University*

McGraw Hill Custom Publishing

Boston   Burr Ridge, IL   Dubuque, IA   Madison, WI   New York   San Francisco   St. Louis
Bangkok   Bogotá   Caracas   Lisbon   London   Madrid
Mexico City   Milan   New Delhi   Seoul   Singapore   Sydney   Taipei   Toronto

2004 PRESIDENTIAL ELECTION

1 2 3 4 5 6 7 8 9 0   DOC   DOC   0 9 8 7 6 5 4

ISBN 0-07-305400-3

Editor: Shirley Grall
Production Editor: Carrie Braun
Printer/Binder: Donnelly & Sons

Reelection campaigns are for incumbents to lose. Voters interview the current job-holder and their challenger to make a decision who should be fired or hired for the position of president, senator, governor or congress member. In particular, the presidential job interview is intense since news coverage and advertising bring the candidates into our homes each day for the most vital choice voters make every four years. In 2004, a majority of voters rehired President George W. Bush (R-TX) with 51 percent of the vote defeating a strong challenge from Senator John Kerry (D-MA) who received 48 percent of the vote. In the Electoral College, President Bush received 286 electoral votes and Senator Kerry 252.

The 2004 presidential election was a national referendum on the job performance of the 43rd president of the United States, George W. Bush. Over the last several decades, polls show that presidents with 50 percent plus job performance ratings never lose reelection. Bill Clinton had a 54 percent rating in 1996 and Ronald Reagan had a 59 percent job approval rating in 1984. George H.W. Bush (R-TX), the president's father lost reelection in 1992 with a presidential job approval rating that hovered around 40 percent the entire election year. His son, George W. Bush had a 53 percent job approval rating in the exit polls taken of voters on election day 2004.[1]

To examine the profound implications of the 2004 election, we examine the political context setting the stage for the presidential campaign, the primary campaign, and the general election campaign. We then proceed to analyze the results of the presidential election, before venturing into a brief review of senate and house elections in 2004.

## Context

The Iraq war and fallout from 9/11 sculpted the political environment for the 2004 election. Domestic issues normally dominate presidential elections. For example, in 1992 a poor economy enabled Governor Bill Clinton (D-AR) to defeat President George H.W. Bush by seven percent. A revived economy enabled President Ronald Reagan (R-CA) to defeat former Vice President Walter Mondale (D-MN) in 1984. The exception was in 1980 when a sliding economy coupled with American embassy personnel held as hostages by Iranian radicals led to the defeat of President Jimmy Carter (D-GA).

### *Iraq*

The war in Iraq had become a protracted fight against guerrilla forces of former Saddam Hussein loyalists and Islamic fundamentalist radicals. The United States along with a division of British forces had swept through the country in a three-week invasion in March and April of 2003 toppling Saddam Hussein from power. While fighting between the United States and the rebels was sporadic through the summer and early fall of 2003, fighting became more intense by November 2003; that month the Iraqi shot down an American-transport helicopter killing 15 American soldiers. The casualty rate continued to climb throughout the winter and an increasingly emboldened enemy challenged the United States. Nevertheless, the process of transferring powers to an Iraqi civilian authority had begun by the spring of 2004 with elections promised by January 2005. American voters had to balance the virtues of establishing a democracy in the Middle East against the cost of over 1100 lives of soldiers in Iraq.

### *Terrorism*

The fight against terrorism remained a major concern for voters following the horrific events of September 11, 2004. A class of new voters emerged called "security moms" identified as white, married women with children, deeply concerned with protecting their families from another terrorist attack. In a *Business Week* article from December 2003, Jennifer Wallace Garner, a 32 year-old mother and self-described social liberal from Northern Virginia said: "I think about a terrorist attack every day…I'm not just thinking about myself anymore. I have my daughter, and I want her to grow up in a safe country." Garner said that unless a Democratic candidate enunciated a "strong and muscular national security policy, she might vote to reelect President Bush." In fact, a poll taken in September 2003 showed that 64 percent of "security moms" favored Bush's reelection almost identical to 66 percent of married men. The threat to a Democratic candidate's base of support was real given that the women's gender gap favored Democratic presidential candidates over Republicans in the recent past, (such as in 2000 when 54 percent of women favored Gore over 43 percent for Bush).[2]

Two additional national issues apart from national security and Iraq set the context for the election: the economy and moral values in American society. Both issues would have profound implications for voters in the 2004 elections.

### The Economy

Economic recovery slowed during late 2003 and early 2004. Employers were not hiring workers at the rate they had during previous economic recoveries—as the unemployment rate stagnated slightly below six percent. Democrats charged that President Bush was the first chief executive since Herbert Hoover (during the Great Depression) to have a net loss of jobs during his term in office. Bush retorted that tax cuts passed by congress, including an eleven year, $1.4 trillion tax relief bill would stimulate consumption, increase economic growth and create jobs. Furthermore, the president argued that 9/11 had contributed to a further economic downturn, since many businesses became cautious given the propensity for market disruption if another terrorist attack occurred. Thus, congress and the president created a Department of Homeland Security to protect the United States against further terrorist attacks by providing it a sizable budget ($34 billion per year). However, slow economic growth and rising health care costs concerned many working class voters in the swing industrial states of Pennsylvania, Ohio and Michigan, casting doubt among them whether the president was truly a good steward of the economy.[3]

### Moral Values

Moral values emerged as a salient factor affecting the 2004 presidential election. Gay marriage and stem cell research became potential "wedge issues"—issues which divide the electorate and influence the campaign's outcome. Christian conservatives favored traditional family values of heterosexual marriage and being pro-life. Social progressives favored civil unions (sometimes gay marriage) and abortion rights.

Gay marriage emerged as an issue when the United States Supreme Court rendered its decision in *Lawrence v. Texas* 539 U.S.C. 558 (2003). The court's majority ruled that cohabiting homosexual couples also have a right to privacy in personal affairs. The decision left open whether gay marriage or civil unions were protected as a fundamental privacy right of citizens. State courts in Massachusetts, Vermont, Alaska and Hawaii "ruled in favor of gay unions." However, "the court rulings were later overridden by state constitutional amendments banning same-sex marriage." Christian conservatives who opposed gay marriage placed proposed state amendments on the ballot of 11 states "codifying marriage as an exclusively heterosexual union." Christian conservatives felt that Democrats were already fostering too permissive a society, and that gay marriage and civil unions was another manifestation of declining moral values they wished to reverse.[4]

President Bush endorsed a constitutional amendment opposing gay marriage in February 2004. On the other hand, Democratic presidential candidates either supported gay marriage or believed that the issue was a state not federal decision.

Stem cell research emerged as a complex issue for pro-life and pro-choice voters. Stem cells have the potential to replicate and repair injuries (such as paralysis) or aid in conquering diseases (such as Parkinson's). Researchers have speculated whether embryonic cells have greater potential than adult stem cells.[5]

The controversy pitted many Christian conservatives against proponents of stem cell research. In an executive decision in 2001, President Bush allowed for the development of 22 existing stem cell lines for scientific research purposes by the federal government, but that no additional adult or embryonic lines should be cultivated.

Bush sought to assure pro-life supporters that the federal government would not permit the cultivation or the extraction of new stem cell lines for scientific research—assuring Catholic conservatives and Christian fundamentalists of his anti-abortion stand. While his supporters were not entirely pleased, the decision promised pro-life advocates that the president shared their concerns about conception. Furthermore, the decision put the president at odds with moderates in his own party and, in particular, Democrats.

Social issues such as abortion and gay marriage alarmed Christian conservatives across the country. Karl Rove, the president's chief political advisor, recommended to George W. Bush never to alienate his political base, which was composed of white, evangelical Christians in the South and Midwest—strong believers in traditional family values. Rove believed that the alienation of the religious fundamentalist political base led to his father's defeat in 1992. George W. Bush, himself a born-again conservative needed little prompting to support these positions, which were consistent with his personal and religious values. The campaign plan was to energize Christian conservatives into a force of supporters that would solidify Bush's support in the most populous regions of the country (again, the South and Midwest).

The backdrop of national security, economic and social issues provided the political context for the 2004 elections. Furthermore, the political polarization between Democrats and Republicans from the 2000 election and the Florida recount controversy, resulting in a 537-vote margin for President Bush in a state of 6.2 million voters still resonated across the country. Strategists in both parties believed the nation remained divided between Democrats and Republicans with few swing voters. Thus, the goal of each party would be to maximize turnout among their respective political bases. For Democrats urban residents, union members, single women, African-Americans, and 18-24 year olds constituted their party base. For Republicans, their base consisted of white men, rural voters, business owners, married couples and religious conservatives. The suburbs and small cities would present the battleground for swing voters determining the outcome of the election.

# Presidential Primaries

President Bush was in a formidable political position entering the 2004 election. Following Republican 2002 midterm election successes creating Republican house and senate majorities and, then the swift defeat of Iraq in April 2003, the president attained a job approval rating of 71 percent according to the Gallup poll. The president stood unchallenged for his party's nomination.[6]

The Democratic field to challenge President Bush opened up in December 2002 when former Vice President Al Gore (D-TN) decided not to compete for his party's presidential nomination following his narrow presidential defeat in 2000. Five major Democrats challenged President Bush: Senator John Kerry (D-MA) a decorated Vietnam War veteran and later, an anti-war activist; freshman Senator John Edwards (D-NC), a former trial lawyer; former governor and populist Howard Dean (D-VT); former House Minority Leader, Rep. Richard Gephardt (D-MO); and, Senator Joseph Lieberman (D-CT), Gore's vice presidential running mate from 2000. The field of major candidates expanded to six when former NATO commander Wesley Clark (D-AR) entered the race in September 2003.

### The Dean Phenomenon

Howard Dean positioned himself as the anti-war candidate of the Democratic party. Known for his fiery oratory and populism, Dean attracted support from left-leaning Democrats yearning for a combative candidate who would be fearless taking on President Bush in the general election. Dean's unabashed anti-Iraq position contrasted with the more cautious positions taken by Kerry, Edwards, Gephardt, and Lieberman. The other four voted to give President Bush the authority to remove Saddam Hussein from power if he failed to eliminate his weapons of mass destruction (WMD) in an October 2002 congressional vote. Dean chided his opponents on the campaign trail and as casualties mounted, the former Vermont governor's argument resonated with more Democrats. Dean raised more than $41 million by January 2004 and his campaign built an organization of 180,000 volunteers.[7]

Dean's meteoric rise as the leading candidate for the Democratic party nomination was stunted when news of Saddam Hussein's capture on December 15, 2003 seemed to strengthen President Bush's hand as a successful commander-in-chief. Many rank-and-file Democrats were less concerned about a populist brand of progressivism offered by Howard Dean and more concerned about finding an "electable" candidate to defeat Bush in the general election. Dean's major competitor in the first nomination contest, the Iowa caucus, was Rep. Richard Gephardt—as both stood at the top of the polls in that state.

Gephardt attacked Dean as an internationally inexperienced governor from a small state not ready to handle the weighty issues of terrorism and war. The pugnacious Dean answered back in his campaign advertising that only a Washington outsider could bring meaningful change to politics in the nation's capital. The tit-for-tat struggle enabled two candidates on the second-tier, John Kerry and John Edwards, to emerge as positive alternatives to Dean and Gephardt. In particular, Kerry organized an impressive field operation that included many Vietnam veterans who were state residents. The Dean campaign brought in an army of volunteers—many from out of state—wearing orange caps. The lower profile approach of the Kerry organization contrasted with the intensity of the Dean volunteers, which played poorly in Iowa—a farm state where modesty, humility and thrift are admired virtues. The Gephardt and Dean campaigns lost ground in the polls as they destroyed each other through television commercials and in sound bites captured on the evening news.

Governor Dean's decline accelerated as he stumbled through a question in an Iowa debate several days before the primary. Reverend Al Sharpton (D-NY), a political activist asked Governor Dean why no minorities served as cabinet officers during his tenure in Vermont (1991-2003) where 97 percent of the residents were white. "Instead of answering the question directly, Dean stated that a senior member of his gubernatorial staff had been a minority. Dean's brusque and evasive answer seemed to contrast with his populist campaign image raising questions about his character and judgment." The former governor's answer only seemed to heighten doubts about his candidacy. Dean's support plunged as his character and temperament became an issue in the campaign. On caucus night, 38 percent of Iowans supported Kerry, 32 percent supported Edwards, 18 percent supported Dean, and 11 percent supported Gephardt. Dean, conceding defeat, exhorted his supporters unaware that national television cameras were recording his words. Dean's "I have a scream" speech was punctuated by a "YEE-AW!" reminiscent of a college coach firing up his team. Dean's visceral reaction to his defeat contrasted with calm concession speeches that are the staple of political campaigns. Dean's unusual reaction raised questions among Democrats whether the former governor was temperamentally suited to be president.[8]

### Kerry Supplants Dean as Frontrunner

The Dean campaign reached a state of collapse the following week when the New Hampshire primary vote gave Kerry another victory (39 percent to Dean's 26 percent). Kerry's emergence as a calm, cool, cautious and experienced politician contrasted with fiery Dean. Edwards, the telegenic youthful senator from North Carolina emerged as Kerry's main opponent, while former General Wesley Clark who did not compete in Iowa, managed to survive the New Hampshire primary finishing third.

Money was pouring into the Kerry campaign as the Dean, Edwards, and Clark campaigns were starving for cash. The Dean campaign had spent all but $5 million by the end of January. Earlier in January, Kerry mortgaged his home for $3.4 million to support his campaign. In two weeks, the Massachusetts senator went from third or fourth place to frontrunner. Success breeds contributions, as the Kerry campaign raised nearly $8 million just in the month of February.[9]

Kerry vanquished his opposition winning 35 out of 38 primaries and caucuses by the end of March 2004. His next task was to transform his campaign from that of a party primary contender to a national political campaign.

*Why Kerry Succeeded*

John Kerry emerged as the Democratic party nominee for two reasons. First, Kerry ran a positive populist campaign articulating a message to fight for ordinary Americans against powerful special interests. Second, the Kerry campaign's advertising focused on the senator's Vietnam War experience offering testimonials from men such as Del Sandusky, a crewmate aboard the swift boat that the Massachusetts senator commanded. Kerry's heroism, valor, and courage sent a powerful message to Democrats seeking to neutralize or minimize President Bush's leadership standing with American voters. Third, Gephardt's advertising strategy ruined Dean's credibility with Iowa voters leaving Kerry as the most "electable" alternative to President Bush.[10]

## General Election Strategy—Bush and Kerry

The strategic goals of campaigns direct the paid advertising, debate strategy, earned media sound bites on the nightly news broadcasts, and deployment of resources to state organizations. Campaigns aim for the coherence of a winnable message and the successful coordination of resources to maximize the influence of that message to key voter groups. The fall campaign started with sixteen contestable states, which later was reduced to eleven competitive state contests: New Hampshire, Florida, Pennsylvania, Ohio, Michigan, Minnesota, Wisconsin, Iowa, New Mexico, Colorado and Nevada. Nearly all the advertising money and resources went into these eleven states by the Bush and Kerry campaigns, which had $75 million apiece of publicly financed money to spend.

*Why Eleven States*

The goal of a presidential campaign is to win 270 electoral votes. Thus, the election represents fifty separate state races (plus the District of Columbia) coordinated by a national campaign organization. Each state awards its electoral votes based on the number of members in its house delegation plus two senators. With the exception of two states (Maine and Nebraska), the winner of the popular vote in the state wins all the electoral votes. For example, Michigan has 15 house members and two senators yielding 17 electoral votes.

The campaign was fought in the eleven states with one-quarter of the nation's population given that 39 states and the District of Columbia were not contestable—meaning that those states were safely in the column of Bush or Kerry. Today, $75 million does not cover the costs of advertising nationally, so that presidential campaigns have to husband their resources, and use them judiciously.

### Bush Strategy and Tactics

Bush's team of advisors, led by White House strategist Karl Rove, campaign manager Ken Mehlman, political director Terry Nelson, and strategist Matthew Dowd, defined the President's strategic goals. Bush ran on his leadership ability during 9/11 and the Iraq war. In essence, the campaign theme of "strong leadership in changing times" implied that a vote for Bush was a vote for political stability. Furthermore, the Bush campaign wanted to underscore that the president was decisive and willing to go to any lengths to protect the American people. Bush's message focused on the Jennifer Wallace Garners of the country, the "security moms" who would normally vote Democratic. Finally, the president exercised message discipline by reiterating the themes of strength and leadership; and the dangers of turning over the ship-of-state during a war against terrorism to an untested newcomer.

Demographically, the Bush campaign sought to increase turnout among religious conservatives, particularly evangelical Christians and conservative Catholics. The strategic architect Karl Rove argued that for Bush to win, Republicans would need to increase their political base by three to four million votes to match the get-out-the-vote (GOTV) effort of Democrats. (Democrats, traditionally, had been more successful in GOTV efforts on election day because of strong organizational efforts by labor unions and large public interest groups to mobilize supporters and get them to the polls). The Bush campaign stressed its secondary theme of protecting moral values by defending marriage as a bond between a man and a woman, and articulating that abortion was a morally wrong choice.

*Kerry Strategy and Tactics*

Coming out of the primaries relatively unscathed, the Kerry campaign examined the polling data and developed a message tying the Democrat's strongest issue of bettering the economy to leadership at home and abroad. Democratic pollster Stan Greenberg and consultant James Carville wrote in a March 25, 2004 memorandum that "the strongest message centers on the aspiration to renew America. The country is desperate for a leader who will prioritize...America's problems and creating a strong country." Again, the theme of strength appeared in the Kerry message of building "a strong America." The Kerry campaign was vying with the Bush campaign for support among the "security moms" while at the same time building a positive prospective message for the future. The purpose was to convince voters that choosing Kerry was just as safe as choosing Bush.[11]

Demographically, the Kerry campaign sought to maintain the base of core Democratic supporters: Jews, African-Americans, single women, labor union members and Hispanics, while growing the level of support among married women and new voters ages 18-24. The strategy to target young college voters was particularly important since many of them opposed the war in Iraq and feared the reinstitution of the draft.

# General Election Campaign

*Phase I—End of the Primaries to the Nominating Conventions*

Phase I (April-July/August 2004) concerned establishing the foundation of how each campaign wished to present its candidate and portray the opponent. Given a financial edge of nearly $108 million during their month of March, the Bush campaign conducted an advertising barrage aimed at raising doubts about Senator Kerry (D-MA) by pointing out inconsistencies in his voting record and statements, especially on Iraq. The Bush strategy of deconstructing Kerry as a weak leader contrasted with the warrior-in-chief President Bush. Bush's attack strategy mirrored the successful Clinton reelection tactic in 1996 of defining the opponent (Bob Dole) before the opponent could define himself. The Clinton campaign portrayed Senator Bob Dole (R-KS) as old, out-of-touch, and too temperamental to be president.[12]

The Kerry campaign had little money to respond on the airwaves in late March and early April, since the senator was busy raising money to fund his campaign through the Democratic convention in late July. The Bush advertising campaign began effectively driving up Kerry's "unfavorable" rating with voters. However, bad news from Iraq and a struggling economy mitigated Kerry's negatives by mid-April. April represented the bloodiest month of the Iraq war as 130 American soldiers died. The news only got worse for the Bush campaign in May when investigative reporter Seymour Hersh uncovered torture conducted by U.S. soldiers against Iraqi prisoners at the Abu Ghraib prison. Furthermore, the Defense Department responded slowly to the Abu Ghraib scandal, which infuriated both congressional Republicans and Democrats.[13]

Data from CBS-New York Times polls from mid-March to late May 2004 demonstrated that bad news reversed the Bush advantage over Kerry. The March 10-14 poll showed Bush with a 46-44 percent lead over Kerry. However, that lead reversed itself in the May 20-23 poll, showing Kerry with a 50-40 percent lead over Bush.[14]

However, by June 2004 the Bush administration regained its footing as casualties in Iraq declined and the United States planned to honor its commitment to hand over political control of Iraq to an interim Prime Minister, Iyad Allawi by the end of June. Allawi would serve until elections took place in January 2005. To the surprise of many observers, Allawi proved himself an able and tough administrator.

The final event of the post-primary season was Kerry's selection of formal rival, Senator John Edwards (D-NC) to be his running mate. Edwards complemented Kerry by providing geographic balance

(North Carolina and Massachusetts) and charisma. He also appealed more to women, working class, and young voters than Kerry, a naturally more stoic politician. Edwards' selection enabled the Kerry campaign to have all its elements in place before the July Convention.

*Phase II—Nominating Convention to Presidential Debates*

Phase II of the general election race featured each campaign's nationally televised advertisement (the national nominating conventions) and continued until the presidential debates. The Democrats held their convention from July 26-29, 2004 in Boston; and, the Republicans held their convention from August 30-September 2, 2004 in New York City. Both conventions had unprecedented security to prevent any potential terrorist attack. Police kept protesting crowds, blocks away from the party conventions.

The Democratic convention told the story of Kerry's military experience. Former generals such as primary rival Wesley Clark and former Chairman of the Joint Chiefs-of-Staff, John Shalikashvili spoke in favor of Kerry's nomination. Kerry, himself was introduced by former Senator and Veterans Administration Chief Max Cleland (D-GA), a triple amputee who served in Vietnam. The most memorable part of Kerry's acceptance speech for the Democratic nomination was his opening line. Kerry saluted the delegates and said, "I'm John Kerry and I'm reporting for duty." The purpose was to portray Kerry as able and tough to handle the war on terrorism and in Iraq.[15]

The Republican national convention highlighted Republican moderates such as former New York Mayor Rudy Giuliani and California Governor Arnold Schwarzenegger. Featuring moderate Republicans was purposeful to attract the support of swing voter groups including "security moms" and NASCAR dads. Furthermore, the Bush campaign sought to avoid alienating swing voters with tough rhetoric (although, keynote speaker Democratic Senator Zell Miller of Georgia came close to undoing the Bush campaign's objectives). Furthermore, the Bush team wanted to make inroads into the senior vote, which had been the province of

Democrats for the last forty years. The moral overtures that the campaign made overtly on stem cell research and gay marriage now expanded to a positive message that imbued all of his policies, including his economic agenda.

Bush stated in his acceptance speech, "I believe we have a moral responsibility to honor America's seniors, so I brought Republicans and Democrats together to strengthen Medicare. Now seniors are getting immediate help buying medicine. Soon every senior will be able to get prescription drug coverage, and nothing will hold us back." Furthermore, the Bush speech laid out an agenda that rhetorically was positive, specific and inclusive. This foundation served Bush well in his fall election campaign because the convention enabled the president to broaden his potential base of support, without alienating his religiously conservative base.[16]

Following the Democratic convention, the Kerry campaign faced a dilemma. Both campaigns received $75 million from the Federal Election Commission to run their fall campaigns. The problem for Kerry and the Democrats was that the party convention finished one month before the Republicans. Thus, the campaign managers for Kerry had one additional month to string out federal funding they received. The Kerry campaign made a strategic decision to minimize expenditures and not engage in a large-scale advertising campaign until mid-September.

Entering the melee of the presidential campaign was the Swift Boat Veterans for Truth (SBVT). In early August 2004, following the Democratic convention and the Kerry campaign stopped its advertising for the reasons mentioned above. SBVT, an independent political group (also known as a 527 group after a section of the tax code) launched a series of advertisements attacking Kerry's service in the Vietnam War and his anti-war protests when he returned home. These veterans served on swift boats in Vietnam as well. The first ad entitled "Any Questions?" doubted Kerry's honesty about his wounds and valor in battle. One swift boat veteran said in the ad, "John Kerry lied to get his bronze star." Another said, "John Kerry betrayed all his shipmates." The power of the advertisement drove down Kerry's personal favorable ratings and his poll ratings, while his campaign was slow to respond. The content of the ads have since been questioned for their veracity, but the "bounce" Kerry received in the polls following the Democratic national convention quickly dissipated given the negative publicity from the Swift Boat advertisements.[17]

*Phase III—Presidential Debates to Closing Weeks of the Campaign*

The fall campaign traditionally starts after Labor Day. The Bush campaign commenced September with a six to ten point lead in public opinion surveys due to a successful convention and the negative effect the swift boat ads had on the Kerry campaign. Through much of September, both campaigns built the foundation for the final push of the campaign by refining their respective messages and state strategies. Advertising by the Bush campaign focused on the president's steadfast leadership following 9/11 and continuing through the war in Iraq. Furthermore, the Bush campaign stressed the idea that Kerry "flip-flopped" on issues and thus, not trustworthy to make definitive decisions. Kerry's advertising sought to rebuild his image as a strong and courageous leader fighting for the interests of the middle class. Both campaign prepared for the three presidential debates and vice presidential debate that would take place during a two-week period from September 30-October 13.

The presidential debates proved to be a boon for the Kerry campaign. Kerry's awkward campaign style (often speaking with a strained voice and waving his arms), was replaced by a cool and confident approach that rattled the president during their first debate. Kerry for the first time clearly articulated his position on Iraq and questioned President Bush's approach of being steadfast and certain in the Iraq war. Kerry stated, "It's one thing to be certain, but you can be certain and wrong." Polls showed Kerry winning the first debate clearly and the last two debates narrowly. Furthermore, the president scowled at Kerry numerous times during the first debate, which seemed to contrast with his sunny, folksy and optimistic presence on the campaign trail. [18]

The debates revived the Kerry campaign, which seemed poised to lose a decisive victory before the October encounters. The president, however, did regain his composure particularly in the last debate, which helped to halt his slide in public opinion surveys. While the debates were a net plus for Kerry, he was still running two to four points behind the president in mid-October.

The frenetic fight to the finish by both campaigns marked the intensity of the campaign. A nation polarized by the 2000 elections and the Iraq was paying intense interest to the campaign. For example, a Pew Center poll compared interest in campaign 2004 to campaign 2000. Fifty-eight percent of survey respondents stated they had "given a lot of thought to the election," compared to 46 percent at the same time four years earlier. Remarkably, the polls compared interest in June of each election year, over four months before the election. By the end of the campaign, approximately 143 million Americans were registered to vote compared to 132.5 million four years earlier—an increase of 10.5 million in the voter rolls.[19]

Despite the negative attacks by both candidates, polls showed little movement following the presidential debate. Bush stabilized his position in the surveys and his communication skills on the campaign trail were superior to the more intellectual, but plodding Kerry. Bush spoke in simple sentences and remained disciplined sticking with his message of not changing course in a time of crisis. Kerry spoke in long and complex sentences that sometimes turned excited crowds into more docile ones. Kerry attacked Bush as a leader who was certain, but often certain and wrong. Kerry attempted to change his theme to a more positive tone in the waning days of the campaign, offering voters "a fresh start." However, the sound bites that appeared on the nightly newscasts from the campaign trail were short bursts of criticism of Bush's Iraq policy. Meanwhile, the Bush campaign reiterated that Kerry was indecisive and not to be trusted in a time of war.[20]

The campaign concluded with two events related to Iraq and the war on terrorism. A cache of 400 tons of explosives were found missing at the Al-Qaqaa facility south of Baghdad. "The disappearance raised questions about why the United States didn't do more to secure the Al-Qaqaa facility" according to the Associated Press. The implication was that tons of explosives were now in the hands of terrorists. However, the military reported later in the week that it had destroyed several hundred tons of explosives near the Al-Qaqaa region. Second, a tape surfaced featuring Osama bin Laden threatening the United States and claiming that the nation would not be safe if either Kerry or Bush was elected president. Bin Laden then proceeded to go into a diatribe about crimes committed by the United States and President Bush. Remarkably, neither event dramatically affected the presidential race, marked by polling stability during the last week of the campaign. Bush maintained a steady 49 percent to 47 percent lead over Kerry when averaging all the major national polls (less than one percent supported independent presidential candidate Ralph Nader).[21]

Both campaigns mobilized voters for their GOTV operation. Labor unions and independent political organizations (known as 527 groups), such as America Coming Together (ACT) and Moveon.org aided the Democrats. Such organizations were spending upwards of $175 million on voter registration and GOTV activities to get supporters to the polls. Eighteen to twenty-nine year old voters were a prime target for GOTV activities by the Kerry campaign to maximize young voter support where polls showed he ran substantially ahead of the president.[22]

Republicans were spending less money than the Democrats (approximately $125 million), yet mobilized a field organization of 1 million volunteers compared to 250,000 for the Democrats. "The Republican strategy - known as the 72 Hour Campaign, referring to a tightly scripted hour-by-hour plan for the final three days - was tested in congressional and local races in 2002, then expanded this year with statewide recruiting and voter registration drives." Each presidential campaign's strategy ended as it began; that the candidate with the better field operation would get out its base of supporters to win the election in a nation with a deeply divided electorate.[23]

# Results

George W. Bush won a clear victory on election day 2004. Bush received 51 percent of the popular vote compared to 48 percent for John Kerry. Bush also won an Electoral College victory with 286 electoral votes compared to 252 for Kerry. Voter turnout exceeded 117 million voters or an increase of nearly 12 million from the 2000 election. Given that increased voter turnout has worked in favor of Democratic presidential candidates in the past, how was Bush able to triumph?

### Security Moms

Exit polling data showed that married women with children voted 40 percent for Kerry and 59 percent for Bush. Even more surprising than the data about "security moms" going 3:2 for Bush was that among all working women—married or unmarried— Kerry received 51 percent of the vote compared to 48 percent for Bush. This marks a sharp gain for Bush compared to 2000, when Gore won the working women's vote by a 58-39 percent margin. Thus, Bush attracted more support from a greater variety of constituent groups than anticipated by political observers.[24]

### Small City Voters

Small city voters, which went for Gore over Bush by a 57-40 percent margin in 2000, broke evenly between Kerry and Bush in 2004 (49-49 percent). For example, turnout in Illinois' centrally located 11th congressional district featuring the small cities of Bloomington and Joliet recorded 258,000 votes in 2000. However, in 2004 the turnout was approximately 295,000. Gore ran one percent behind Bush in the district in 2000, while Kerry ran 11 percent behind Bush in the same district in 2004. Small Midwestern cities tended to strongly support Bush. In these areas, the Republican GOTV operation made the biggest difference enabling the president to win Ohio and Iowa—and narrow the margin of Kerry victories in Pennsylvania, Michigan, Minnesota and Wisconsin.[25]

*Turnout Among 18-29 Year Olds*

According to Harvard University's Kennedy School of
Government survey, 20 million young voters cast ballots in 2004
compared to 15.4 million in 2000. Kerry carried the age cohort
with a plurality of 11 percent, or by approximately 2.2 million
voters. Gore carried the same cohort by two percent in 2000 or
approximately 300,000 voters. Thus, young voters helped the
Kerry campaign win support, but not enough to overcome the
plurality of 3.5 million votes in Bush's favor.[26]

*No Dominant Issue*

No single issue dominated voters' decision making in 2004. A
plurality of voters named moral values (22 percent), followed
closely by the economy/jobs (20 percent), terrorism (19 percent)
and Iraq (15 percent). The lack of a dominant issue in the
campaign benefits the incumbent since there is no single issue for
angry voters to coalesce around to oppose them in large numbers.[27]

*Turnout Among Evangelicals Increases*

The white evangelical/born-again Christian vote, which comprised
23 percent of the electorate, gave Bush a 57-point margin over
Kerry. In fact, the same group of voters comprised only 14 percent
of the electorate in 2000 according to exit poll surveys indicating a
massive nine percentage point increase among the entire electorate.
(However, the 2000 exit poll question was framed more narrowly,
which may have understated evangelical-born again participation
by one or three percent). The results did demonstrate how
effective the Bush campaign was in getting Christian conservatives
out to vote. Furthermore, Bush won the Catholic vote in 2004—
the first time a Republican has ever won the Catholic vote in a
tightly contested presidential election.[28]

*Bush Wins on the Economy*

The economy was Kerry's strongest issue in the campaign. Yet,
when voters were asked in the exit poll "who would you trust to
handle the economy," 40 percent preferred Bush, 38 percent

preferred Kerry, 8 percent reported both, and 13 percent stated neither of them. Bush won every major issue area over Kerry, when the word "trust" framed the question. The Bush campaign effectively articulated that the president had the better morals and values, which are corollaries of trust; and that permeated voter decision making on all issues, not just wedge social issues such as gay marriage.[29]

*Florida, Pennsylvania and Ohio*

The big three swing states to determine the election had 68 electoral votes among them. Florida (27 electoral votes) went for Bush by a surprisingly wide margin of 52-47 percent or approximately 350,000 votes. One might attribute the margin to the federal government's rapid hurricane relief during the month of September when four consecutive storms ravaged the state. Pennsylvania (21 electoral votes) trends toward Democrats because the two large cities on the bookends of the state (Pittsburgh and Philadelphia) are so strongly Democratic, that they counteract the Republican margin in the central part of the state. President Bush made over 40 trips to the state, but massive turnout in the Philadelphia and Pittsburgh areas enabled Kerry to carry the state by a 51-49 percent margin. Ohio (20 electoral votes) appeared to be the closest of the swing states and a better opportunity for a Kerry win than Florida. However, the presence of a state amendment preventing same-sex marriage may have energized evangelicals and fundamentalists to vote on election day. The amendment passed by a 3:2 margin, while Bush defeated Kerry by 136,000 votes in a state where 5.4 million cast votes on election day.

*Summary*

Relative satisfaction with a sitting president (53 percent approval rating), a massive increase among white evangelical/born-again Christian voters participating in the election, and winning the Catholic vote led to the Bush victory. This mitigated any increase for Kerry among young voters. Furthermore, Bush almost neutralized the gender gap (with Kerry winning women voters over

Bush by three percent).  The data seem to indicate a strong argument for Bush winning the election.[30]

## Senate Races

Democrats faced an uphill struggle to regain control of the Senate in 2004.  Democratic senators from Florida, Georgia, Louisiana, North Carolina and South Carolina retired.  In each state (with the exception of Florida, an even race) Republicans were favored to win the senate seats.  Republicans won each seat, including Florida giving them a pickup of five seats in the south.  Furthermore, Senate Minority Leader Tom Daschle (D-SD) was in the fight for his political career against former Congressman John Thune (R), an attractive, intelligent and telegenic candidate.  Thune had lost his previous senate bid to incumbent Democrat Tim Johnson in 2002 by only 527 votes.  Higher voter turnout in a predominantly Republican state (South Dakota) enabled Thune to defeat Daschle by a 51-49 percent margin, clearly the biggest victory for Republicans aside from the presidency in 2004.  The candidates spent $26 million between them or about $50 per voter.[31]

Two Democrats Barack Obama (D) and Ken Salazar (D) won seats vacated by Republican retirees in, respectively, Illinois and Colorado.  Obama, who delivered the rousing keynote address at the Democratic National convention, represented one of the few bright moments for Democrats on election night.

The most peculiar senate contest took place in Kentucky where incumbent Republican Jim Bunning (R) almost lost his seat to physician Daniel Mongiardo (D).  Bunning's mental stability became an issue in the campaign.  "At one event, Bunning said Mongiardo, whose roots are Italian, looked like one of Saddam Hussein's sons, known for their murderous ways."  Bunning also failed to appear at a debate with Mongiardo in Kentucky.  However, he appeared in a Republican studio from Washington, and apparently read answers to reporter questions from a teleprompter.  Finally, Bunning traveled with a state trooper late in the campaign claiming, "there might be strangers among us." Bunning squandered a 20-point lead in the polls during the last three weeks of the campaign, but was able to squeak by with a 51-49 percent win in a strong Republican state.[32]

The night was a success for Republicans as they increased their senate majority by four seats (51 to 55) seats. The new senate would consist of 55 Republicans, 44 Democrats and 1 Independent (James Jeffords of Vermont who caucuses with the Democrats).

## House Races

The 2004 elections marked the fifth consecutive election where little turnover occurred in the House of Representatives. Approximately, 98 percent of house incumbents won reelection. Republicans increased their majority in the house by at least a four-seat margin, giving them 231 seats to 201 for the Democrats and 1 independent (Socialist Bernie Sanders of Vermont who caucuses with the Democrats). Two undecided Louisiana seats were subject to a runoff in December because no candidate won a majority on election day. (Louisiana runs its election system differently from every other state). Redistricting in Texas by the Republican legislature provided a major boost for Republicans. Three Democratic incumbents lost (Max Sandlin, Nick Lampson and Martin Frost), while one redistricted Democrat (Chet Edwards) held on to victory. Republicans picked up five seats in Texas alone.[33]

## Campaign Spending

Despite passage of a new campaign finance law in 2002, federal campaign spending accelerated upwards of $3.9 billion in 2004—an increase of $900 million from 2000. The Center for Responsive Politics, which monitors campaign expenditures, reported that Bush and Kerry spent $617 million together, in their bid for the White House. Spending by independent groups and parties in the presidential race (on advertisement and GOTV) increased overall expenditures to $1.2 billion (about 30 percent of spending on all federal races). Furthermore, spending by 527 groups, which are independent political organizations not affiliated with candidates or parties, approximated $386 million in the 2004 elections. The new campaign finance law did not curtail spending, which was one objective of proponents.[34]

## The 2004 Elections and Implications for the Future

The 2004 elections established the Republican party as the majority party in the United States. While the nation remained deeply divided, Republicans increased their representation in the house and senate. Furthermore, the president won a majority of the popular vote in 2004, unlike the 2000 election. President Bush claimed the election gave him a mandate to bring about sweeping change to the tax code, and to begin privatizing part of the social security system. The prospect of replacing several key members of the Supreme Court provided the president an opportunity to shape the court closer to his ideology—a belief in limited not activist judicial power. It also bought the president time to establish a democracy in Iraq. Whether the president succeeds or fails depends on how successful Democrats are in thwarting his policies, the state of the economy, the course of events in Iraq, and the propensity of terrorist organizations such as Al-Queda to strike successfully again in the United States.

### The 2008 Elections--Republicans

Republicans are already lining up to succeed President Bush. Vice President Dick Cheney has stated that he will not run for president in 2008, nor will Governor Jeb Bush (R-FL), announcing he will not run to succeed his brother. Republican Majority Leader Bill Frist (R-TN) has signaled his interest in running, as has Senator Chuck Hagel (R-NE), a Vietnam veteran from the moderate wing of the party. Senator John McCain (R-AZ) who ran an unsuccessful, but competitive race against Bush in the 2000 Republican presidential primaries is also considering a bid. Four of the last five individuals elected president (Jimmy Carter, Ronald Reagan, Bill Clinton and George W. Bush) served as governors. Republican governors such as George Pataki (R-NY), Bill Owens (R-CO), Mitt Romney (R-MA), and Tim Pawlenty (R-MN) are possible candidates. Former New York City Mayor Rudy Giuliani, however, appears to be leading in early polls for the 2008 Republican nomination.[35]

Senator Hillary Rodham Clinton (D-NY) is the clear favorite among Democrats who might contend in 2008. Her massive fund raising base and network of national support across the nation give her a tremendous advantage in terms of resources and name recognition. Senator John Kerry (D-MA) is unlikely to run again. The plans of former Vice President Al Gore (D-TN) are unknown at this time. Vice presidential candidate John Edwards (D-NC) might attempt another bid for the Democratic party nomination. Other Democrats considering a run for the White House include Governor Tom Vilsack (D-IA), Governor Mark Warner (D-VA), Governor Bill Richardson (D-NM) and Senator Evan Bayh (D-IN).

The race is now on for the presidential election in 2008. The final chapter of the Bush presidency will help determine the political environment over the next four years. Prospective candidates have begun preliminary planning and political observers have begun their speculation...only days after the 2004 election!

---

**NOTES**

[1] NEP election day survey, November 2, 2004 on Bush job approval. Gallup Opinion poll data on Clinton job approval rating, 1996. ABC News survey data, 1984 Reagan approval rating. Gallup Opinion Index survey data, George H.W. Bush average approval rating, 1992.

[2] Alexandra Starr, "Security Moms": An Edge for Bush?" *BusinessWeekonline*. Accessed on November 5, 2004 from www.businessweek.com. Web page edition, December 1, 2003. Gore-Bush gender gap data from Voter News Service, exit poll, November 7, 2000. Accessed on December 28, 2000. Reported from www.cnn.com.

[3] Department of Homeland Security. Fiscal year budget for 2005 is $33.8 billion. Accessed from www.whitehouse.gov/omb/budget on November 10, 2004.

[4] Kavan Peterson, "50-state rundown on gay marriage laws," *Stateline.org*. Accessed on November, 5, 2004 from www.stateline.org. Web page edition, November 3, 2004.

[5]"Stem Cell Information," National Institutes of Health, United States Government. Accessed on November 4, 2004 from www.stemcells.nih.gov. Web page edition, June 11, 2004. Web page accessed on basics of how stem cell research works.

[6] Gallup poll, April 14-16, 2003. Sample size 1,011 adults reported in www.pollingreport.com. Accessed on November 5, 2003.

[7] The Dean campaign had 186,000 volunteers and organizers as of January 30, 2004 according to www.meetup.com. Sharon Thiemer, "Howard Dean's Sees Campaign Funds Dwindle As Losses Mount; John Kerry Reaps Benefits of Victory," *Associated Press*, January 30, 2004, on Dean campaign finances. See also Richard J. Semiatin, *Campaigns in the 21st Century*, (New York: McGraw-Hill 2005, 235-238) on the 2004 presidential primaries.

[8] Semiatin, ibid, 237.

[9] Thiemer, ibid on Dean resources. Kerry contribution data from "John Kerry—Campaign Finances," compiled by Eric M. Appleman from Center for Responsive Politics and Center for Public Integrity data. February and March 2004 reports by the Kerry campaign. Accessed on November 5, 2004 from www2.gwu.edu.

[10] Semiatin, ibid, 238.

[11] Stan Greenberg and James Carville, "First Engagement: Notes on the Latest Democracy Corps Poll," Democracy Corps, March 25, 2004, 2.

[12] Eric Appleman, ibid, Kerry. "George W. Bush—Campaign Finances," compiled by Eric M. Appleman from Center for Responsive Politics and Center for Public Integrity data. March 2004 report by the Bush campaign. Accessed on November 5, 2004 from www2.gwu.edu.

[13] See Seymour M. Hersh, "Torture at Abu Ghraib," *The New Yorker*, May 10, 2004. Department of Defense (DoD) and Central Command (CENTCOM) provide official data on U.S. casualties.

[14] CBS News-New York Times polls of March 10-14, 2004 and May 20-23, 2004 were conducted with registered voters with a plus three or four percent error margin.

[15] "Kerry hits the road after convention address," *USA Today*, July 31, 2004. Accessed on November 5, 2004 from www.usatoday.com. Web page edition July 31, 2004.

[16] "President Bush's Acceptance Speech to the Republican National Convention," September 2, 2004, New York. Text accessed from www.cnn.com on November 6, 2005.

[17] "Any Questions?" Swift Boat Veterans for Truth. Produced by Stevens, Reed, Curcio and Potham, Alexandria, VA. Ad debuted August 5, 2004. Accessed on November 6, 2004 from www2.gwu.edu, web page edition.

[18] See Tom Curry, "Bush, Kerry clash over History, Allies," from www.msnbc.com. Web page edition, October 1, 2004. Accessed on November 6, 2004.

[19] "Voters More Engaged, But Campaign Gets Lukewarm Ratings," Pew Research Center poll, June 3-13, 2004. Released on July 8, 2004. Accessed from www.people-press.org on November 6, 2004, web page edition. Jim Drinkard, "Wave of Voters, Vote Watchers, Building," *USA Today*, October 28, 2004. Web page edition updated, October 29, 2004. Accessed from www.usatoday.com on November 6, 2004 regarding voter registration.

[20] For information on a "fresh start" go to www.johnkerry.com. Web page, edition, October 14, 2004. Accessed on November 6, 2004.

[21] William J. Kole, "U.N.: 400 Tons of Iraq Explosives Missing," *The Associated Press*, October 26, 2004. Kirk Johnson, "Voters, Their Minds Made Up, Say bin Laden Changes Nothing," *The New York Times*, October 31, 2004. Accessed on November 6, 2004 from www.nytimes.com, web page edition. Average of polls from www.realpolitics.com. Accessed on October 25-November 2, 2004.

[22] Dan Balz and Thomas B. Edsall, "Unprecedented Efforts to Mobilize Voters Begin, *The Washington Post*, November 1, 2004, A1.

[23] James Dao, "To Get Ohio Voters to the Polls, Volunteers Knock, Talk and Cajole," *The New York Times*, November 1, 2004, web page edition. Accessed on November 6, 2004 from www.nytimes.com. Dan Balz and Thomas B. Edsall, ibid on number of volunteers and money spent by both parties.

[24] National exit poll, consortium of ABC, CBS, NBC, CNN, Fox and the Associated Press, conducted by Mitofsky International, November 2, 2004 with 13,660 respondents. Web page updated November 3, 2004. Accessed on November 4, 2004 from www.cnn.com. Voter News Service exit poll, consortium (same as above), November 7, 2000 with 13,130 respondents. Web page updated November 8, 2000. Accessed on February 1, 2001 from www.cnn.com.

[25] NEP ibid, VNS ibid. Election data from Michael Barone with Richard E. Cohen, *The Almanac of American Politics 2004* (Washington, D.C.: National Journal, 2003) p.562, on 2000 turnout from Illinois' 11th congressional district.

[26] Martha Irvine, "Banner Youth Vote Diluted By Big Overall Turnout, but Experts Still Find Results Encouraging," *The Associated Press*, November 6, 2004.

[27] NEP, ibid.

[28] NEP, ibid. VNS 2000 ibid.

[29] NEP, ibid.

[30] NEP, ibid.

[31] "Republicans Hold Control of the Senate," *The Associated Press*, November 2, 2004.

[32] Peter Slevin, "Incumbent's Gaffes Narrow Ky. Senate Race," *The Washington Post*, October 21, 2004, A7.

[33] Election results data from www.msnbc.com accessed on November 6, 2004. Web page edition updated November 3, 2004.

[34] "'04 Elections Expected To cost Nearly $4 Billion," press release, Center for Responsive Politics, Washington, D.C., October 21, 2004. Accessed on November 4, 2004 from www.opensecrets.org.

[35] McLaughlin and Associates poll, conducted November 2, 2004 with 1,000 general election voters. Reported on www.pollingreport.com. Accessed on November 6, 2004.